EAGLES ILLUSTR.

Allies in the Pacific

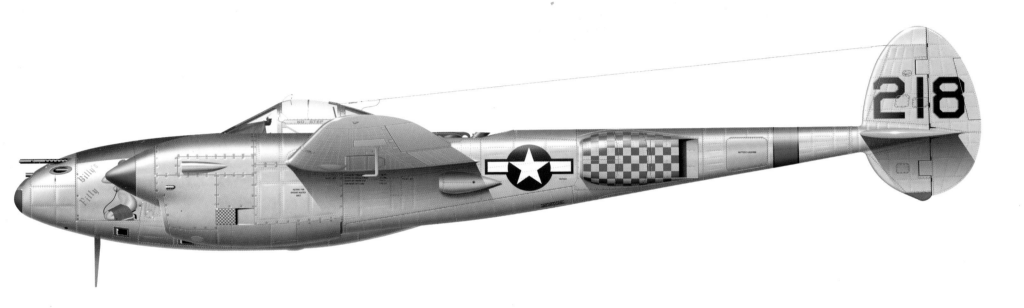

by Thomas A. Tullis

eagle
EDITIONS LTD.

Curtiss Hawk H81A-2 (P-40B)

Fin # P-8186
William Reed • 3rd Pursuit Squadron, American Volunteer Group (A.V.G.) • China • 1941

Notes:
The upper surface pattern was applied using rubber templates resulting in a fairly hard edged camouflage similar to RAF fighters.
Several extremely detailed photos of this aircraft were obtained for this illustration, but none showed the fuselage number.
This was reconstructed based on other AVG aircraft with those numerals and the '75' on the mid fuselage, all of which matched perfectly.
Note the original chalk sketches on the cowl for the painting of the shark's mouth. At least two other designs are visible besides the final painted one.
For their group's courage, duty, innovation, and tenacity in the face of adversity, the AVG Flying Tigers were the recipients of the
National Aviation Hall of Fame's 1999 "Milton Caniff Spirit of Flight Award."

Colors:
Undersurfaces: Sky (actually a DuPont color which was a cool grey with a slight bluish-green hue-not a very good match for the British Sky color)
Uppersurfaces: Dark Earth, Dark Green
Prop blades: Black with Yellow tips

References:
Original photos

Lockheed P-38L-1

s/n: 44-24155 • Maj. Tom McGuire • CO 431st FS, 475th FG • Philippines • Late 1944

Notes:
McGuire was a recipient of the Medal of Honor for his bravery, and his final score was 38 victories.
The 'Iron Major', as he was called, was killed in action over the island of Negros on 7 January 1945.
Tom McGuire was enshrined into the National Aviation Hall of Fame in 2000.

Colors:
Overall natural metal with some areas painted aluminum
Prop Blades: Black with Yellow tips
Anti-glare panel: Black

References:
Possum, Clover & Hades: The 475th Fighter Group in WWII by John Stanaway. Schiffer Publishing, 1993.
Interview with John Stanaway.

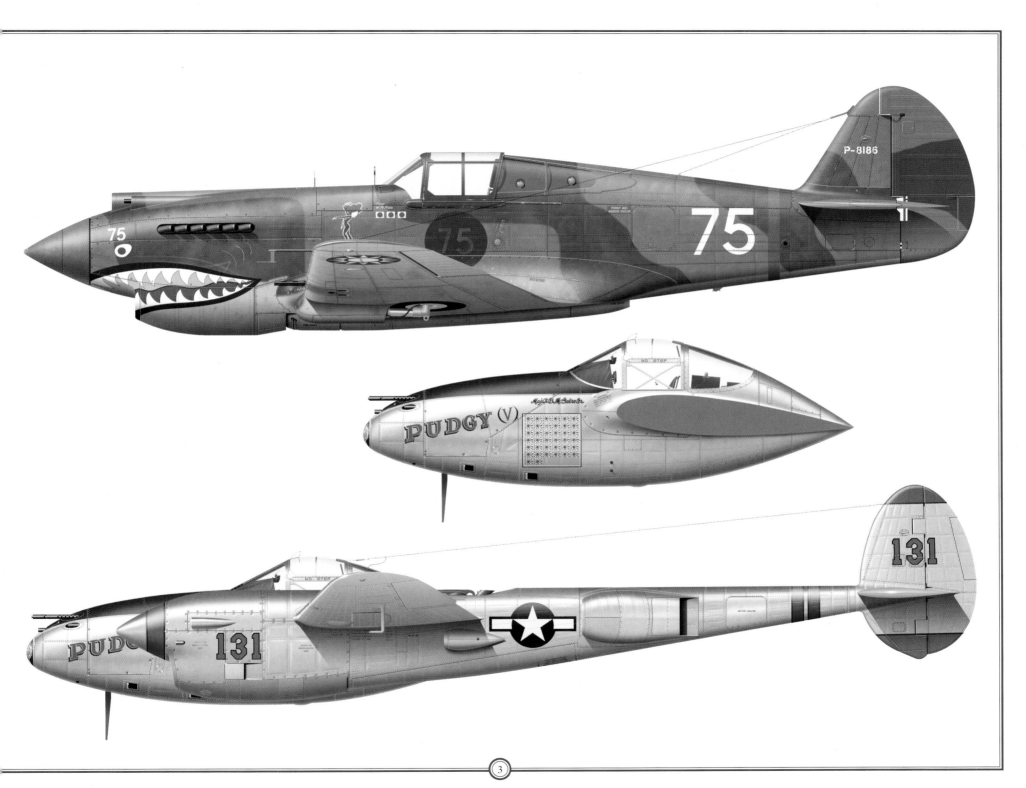

Curtiss Hawk H81A-2 (P-40B)

Fin # P-8194
Robert Neale • 1st Pursuit Squadron, American Volunteer Group (A.V.G.) • China • 1941

Notes:
The upper surface pattern was applied using rubber templates resulting in a fairly hard edged camouflage similar to RAF fighters.
For their group's courage, duty, innovation, and tenacity in the face of adversity, the AVG Flying Tigers were the recipients of the
National Aviation Hall of Fame's 1999 "Milton Caniff Spirit of Flight Award."

Colors:
Undersurfaces: Sky
Uppersurfaces: Dark Earth, Dark Green
Prop blades: Black with Yellow tips

References:
Original photos

Vought F4U-1A

NZ5326 • RNZAF • 1944

Notes:
Note the dark paint that has been applied on the forward fuselage. This has been interpreted as a Dark Blue, similar to that used by the U.S. Navy.
While many F4Us in the RNZAF retained their U.S. Navy colors, some RNZAF Corsairs were repainted in a medium Blue Gray color over Light Gray.

Colors:
Fuselage & Wings: Blue Gray over Light Gray.
Prop Blades: Black with Yellow tips

References:
Corsair Aces of World War 2 by Mark Styling. Osprey Publishing, 1995.
F4U Corsair, Monografie #11. A-J Press, 1993.

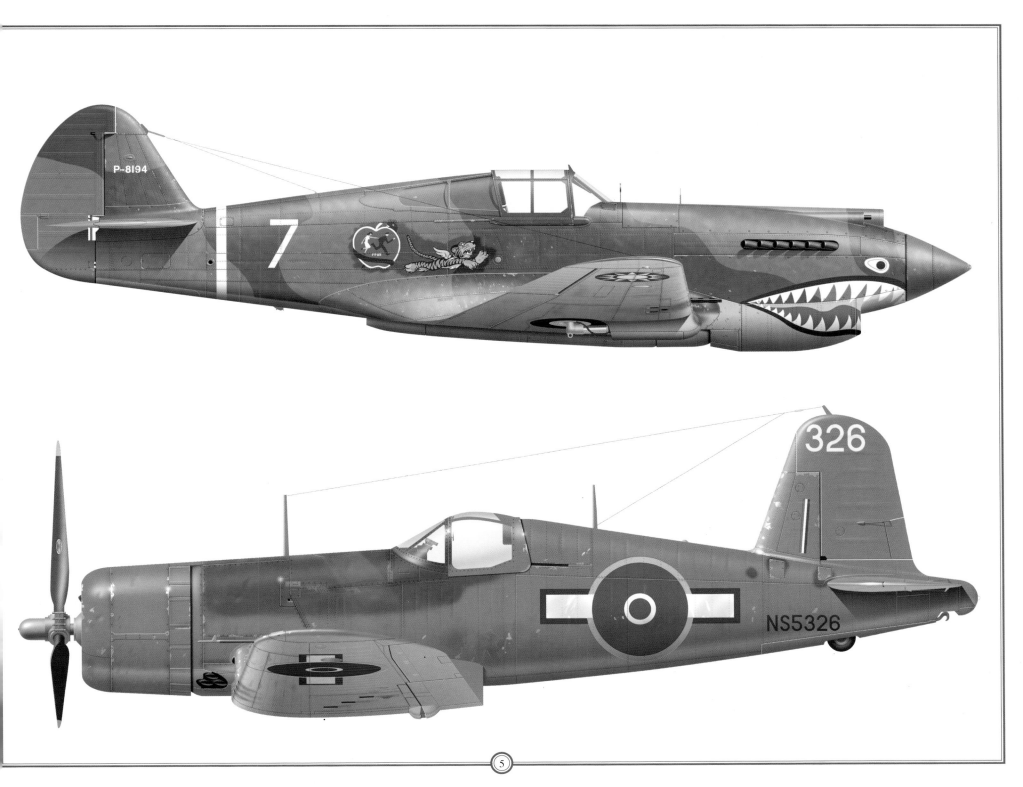

Grumman F4F-4

Capt. Joe Foss • VMF-121 • Guadalcanal • October 1942

Notes:
This profile is provisional based on information provided by Foss.
Black 53 was one of several Wildcats flown by Foss.
Foss ended the war with 26 confirmed victories, and was later elected Governor of South Dakota.
General Joseph Jacob Foss was enshrined into the National Aviation Hall of Fame in 1984.

Colors:
Standard U.S. Navy two tone scheme consisting of Blue Gray over Light Gray
Prop Blades: Black with Yellow tips

References:
Interview with General Joe Foss

Vought F4U-1

1st Lt. Foy R. Garrison • VMF-213 • Guadalcanal • July 1943

Notes:
Only the forward fuselage was visible in the reference photo. The style and placement of the fuselage number
is based on other aircraft in the same unit at the same time.

Colors:
Standard U.S. Navy two tone scheme consisting of Blue Gray over Light Gray
Prop Blades: Black with Yellow tips

References:
Corsair Aces of World War 2 by Mark Styling. Osprey Publishing, 1995.

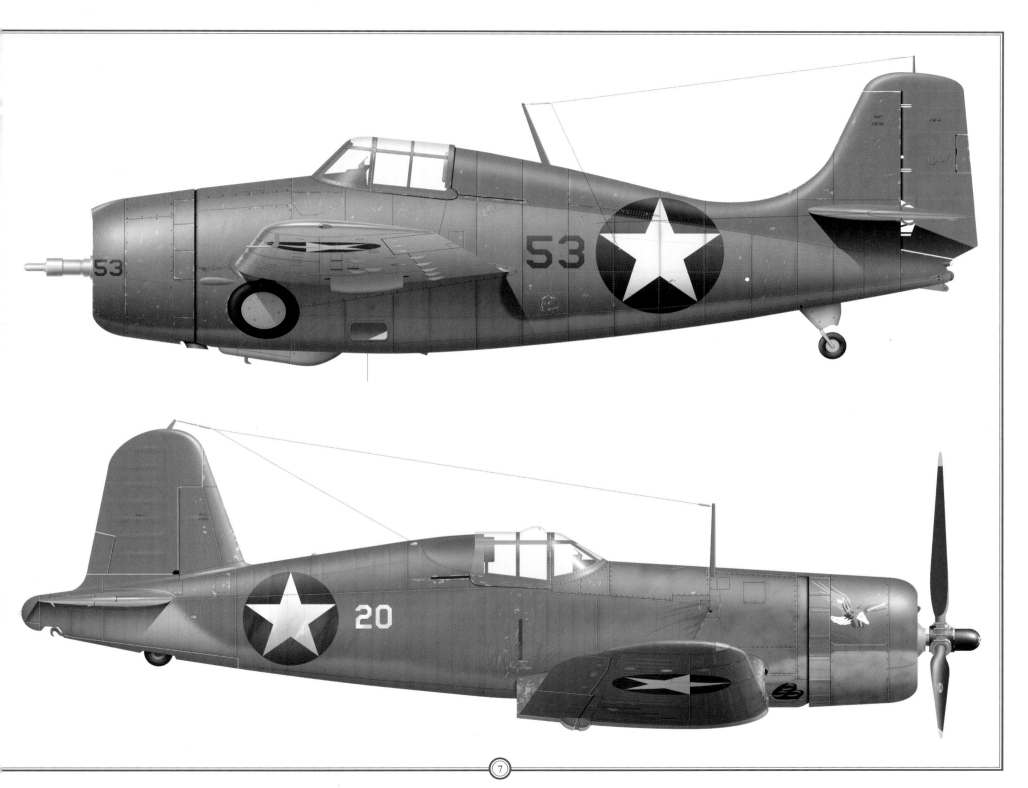

North American P-51D-20-NA

"Squirt" s/n: 44-63423 • James Beckwith, Commander 15th FG

Colors:
Overall natural metal
Spinner: Yellow and Black • Prop Blades: Black with Yellow tips
Identification markings: Black with Yellow edge stripes
Anti-glare panel: Olive Drab

References:
Air Force Colors Vol. 3 by Dana Bell. Squadron/Signal Publications, 1998

Vought F4U-1A

NZ5315 • RNZAF • 1944

Notes:
Note the dark paint that has been applied on the forward fuselage. This has been interpreted as a Dark Blue, similar to that used by the U.S. Navy.
While many F4Us in the RNZAF retained their U.S. Navy colors, some RNZAF Corsairs were repainted in a medium Blue Gray color over Light Gray.

Colors:
Fuselage & Wings: Blue Gray over Light Gray.
Prop Blades: Black with Yellow tips

References:
Corsair Aces of World War 2 by Mark Styling. Osprey Publishing, 1995.
F4U Corsair, Monografie #11. A-J Press, 1993.

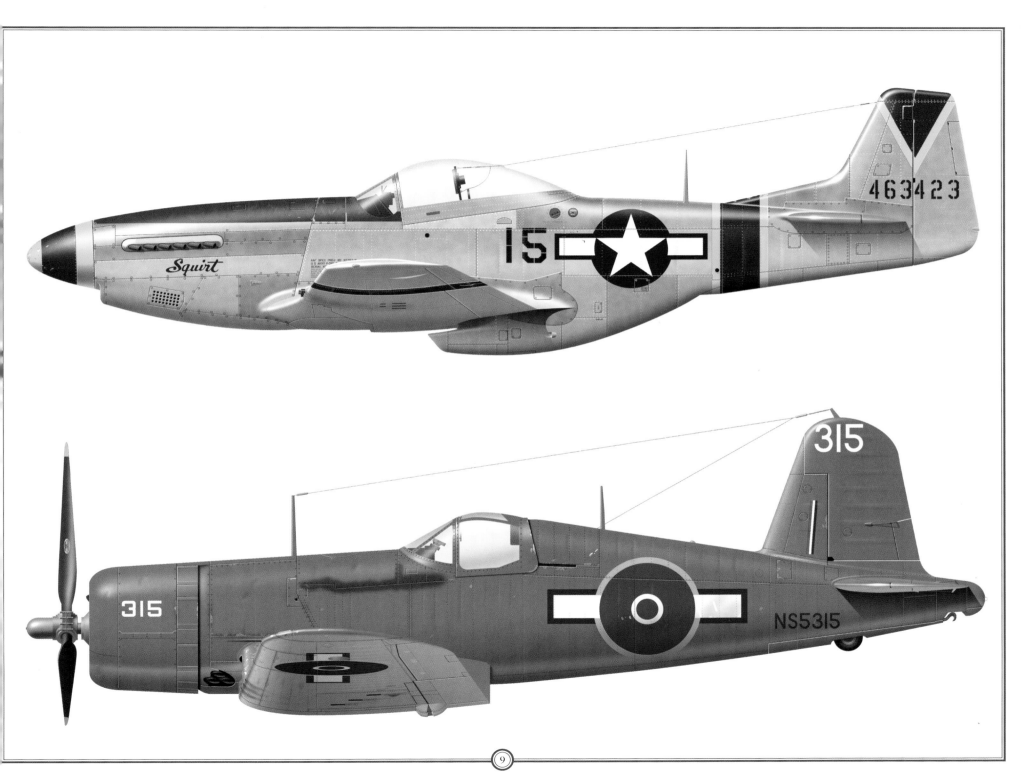

Curtiss Hawk H81A-2 (P-40B)

Fin # P-8103
Dick Rossi • 1st Pursuit Squadron, American Volunteer Group (A.V.G.) • China • 1941

Notes:
The upper surface pattern was applied using rubber templates resulting in a fairly hard edged camouflage similar to RAF fighters.
The shark's mouth is provisional as no photos of this aircraft after the shark's mouth had been applied could be found.
For their group's courage, duty, innovation, and tenacity in the face of adversity, the AVG Flying Tigers were the recipients of the
National Aviation Hall of Fame's 1999 "Milton Caniff Spirit of Flight Award."

Colors:
Undersurfaces: Sky (actually a DuPont color which was a cool grey with a slight bluish-green hue-not a very good match for the British Sky color)
Uppersurfaces: Dark Earth, Dark Green
Prop blades: Black with Yellow tips

References:
Original photos & interviews with Dick Rossi

Lockheed P-38L

"Miss Cheri" • 80th FS, 8th FG • Ie Shima • April-July 1945

Colors:
Overall natural metal with some areas painted aluminum
Prop Blades: Black with Yellow tips
Anti-glare panel: Olive Drab

References:
Attack & Conquer: The 8th Fighter Group in WWII by John Stanaway. Schiffer Publishing, 1995.
Interview with John Stanaway.

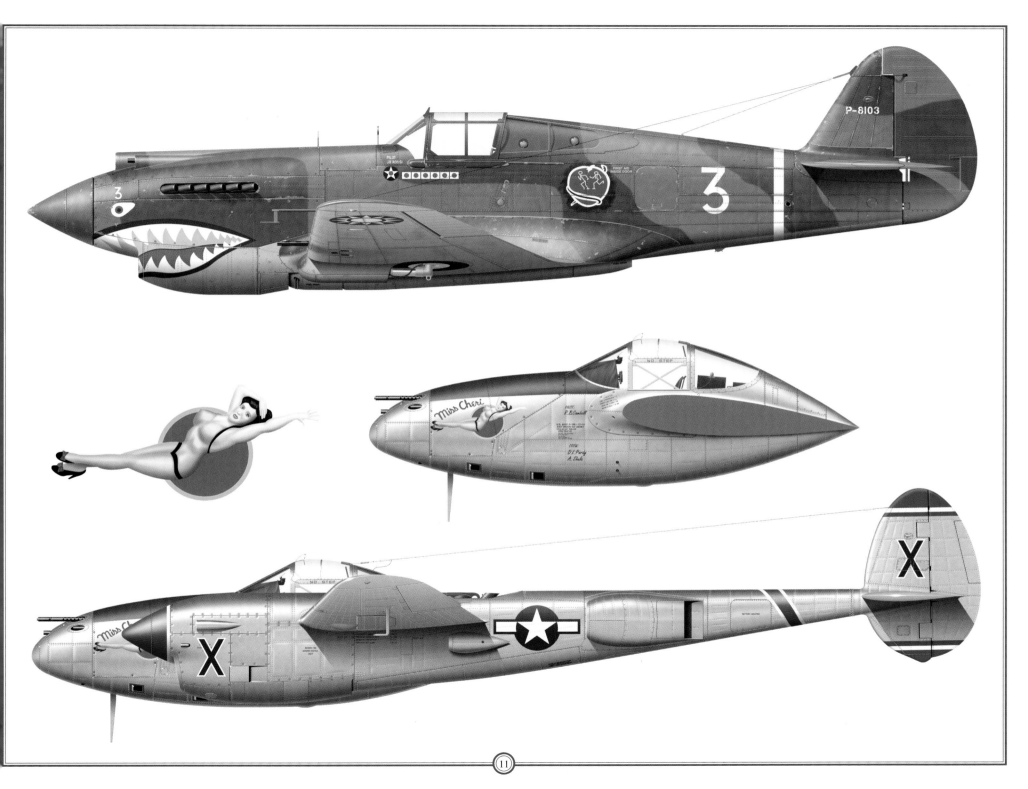

Vought F4U-1D

VMF-312 • June 1945

Notes:
Note that the dark checks on the cowl and tail are Glossy Sea Blue, not Black as sometimes depicted.
This F4U-1D has the old style braced canopy that was common to F4U-1A Corsairs.

Colors:
Standard U.S. Navy Glossy Sea Blue scheme
Prop Blades: Black with Yellow tips

References:
F4U Corsair in action (original edition) by Jim Sullivan. Squadron Signal Publications, 1977.

North American P-51D-20-NA

s/n: 44-64055 • 3rd ACG • 1945

Notes:
Note that the area between the two black fuselage stripes has been painted white.

Colors:
Overall natural metal
Spinner: Yellow • Prop Blades: Black with Yellow tips
Anti-glare panel: Olive Drab

References:
Osprey Aircraft of the Aces #26 Mustang & Thunderbolt Aces of the Pacific & CBI by John Stanaway. Osprey Publishing Ltd. 1999.

Vought F4U-1

"MARINE'S DREAM" • BuNo: 02576 • 1st Lt. Edwin L. Olander • VMF-214 • Munda • October 1943

Colors:
Standard U.S. Navy two tone scheme consisting of Blue Gray over Light Gray
Prop Blades: Black with Yellow tips

References:
Original photos from the collection of Jim Sullivan.
Corsair Aces of World War 2 by Mark Styling. Osprey Publishing, 1995.
F4U-Corsair in Color by Jim Sullivan. Squadron Signal Publications, 1981.

Curtiss P-40C

s/n: 41-13297 • 18th Pursuit Group • Wheeler Field, Hawaii • 26 October 1941

Notes:
Buzz number is different than serial number.
Underwing 'U.S. ARMY' was actually Insignia Blue, not Black as often depicted.
This aircraft had the two filler caps on the upper fuselage behind the cockpit glass,
not on the fuselage side as was common on other 'C' models.

Colors:
Undersurfaces: Neutral Grey
Uppersurfaces: Olive Drab
Prop blades: Black with Yellow tips

References:
Original Photos

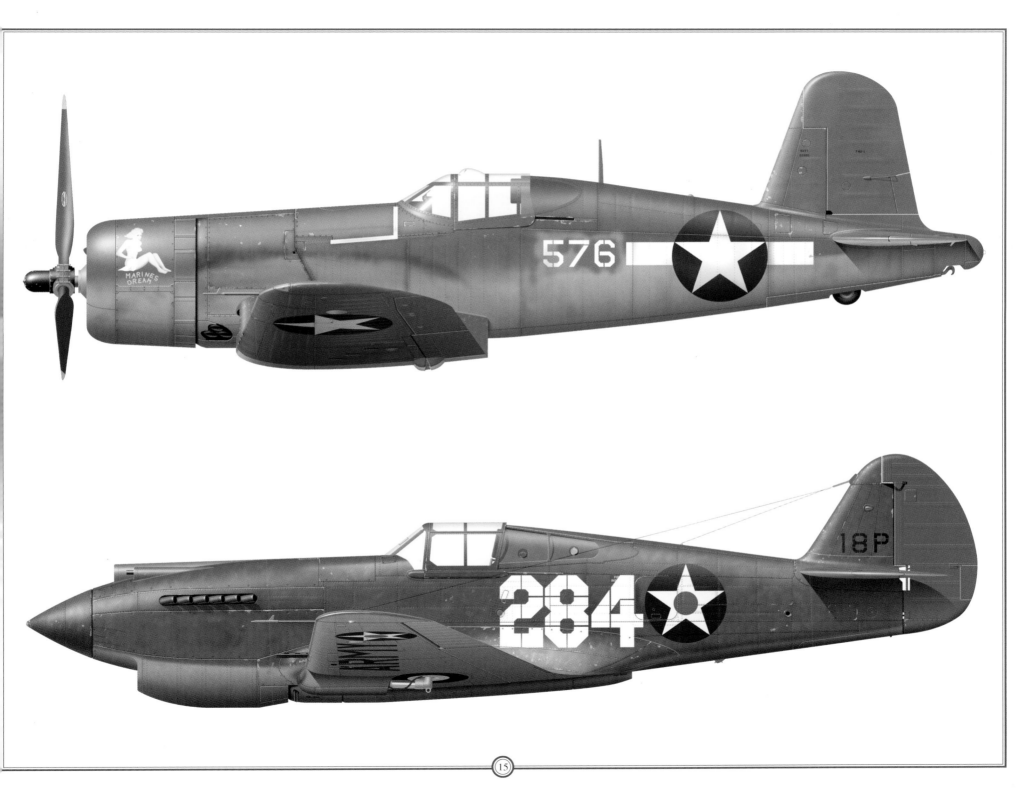

Lockheed P-38L-1

Lt. William Fowkes • 12th FS, 18th FG • Zamboanga, Philippines

Colors:
Overall natural metal with some areas painted aluminum
Prop Blades: Black with Yellow tips
Spinner: Medium Blue
Squadron markings: Medium Blue checkers and trim
Anti-glare panel: Olive Drab

References:
P-38 Lightning in Detail and Scale by Bert Kinzey. Squadron Signal Publications, 1998.
P-38 Lightning in WWII Color by Jeff Ethell. Motorbooks, 1994.

Vought F4U-1A

Lt. D. Cunningham • VF-17

Colors:
Standard U.S. Navy tri-color scheme consisting of Non Specular Sea Blue, Intermediate Blue and Non Specular White
Prop Blades: Black with Yellow tips

References:
Markings of the Aces, US NAVY Book 2 by Charles Graham & Richard Hill. Kookaburra Technical Pub., 1972.

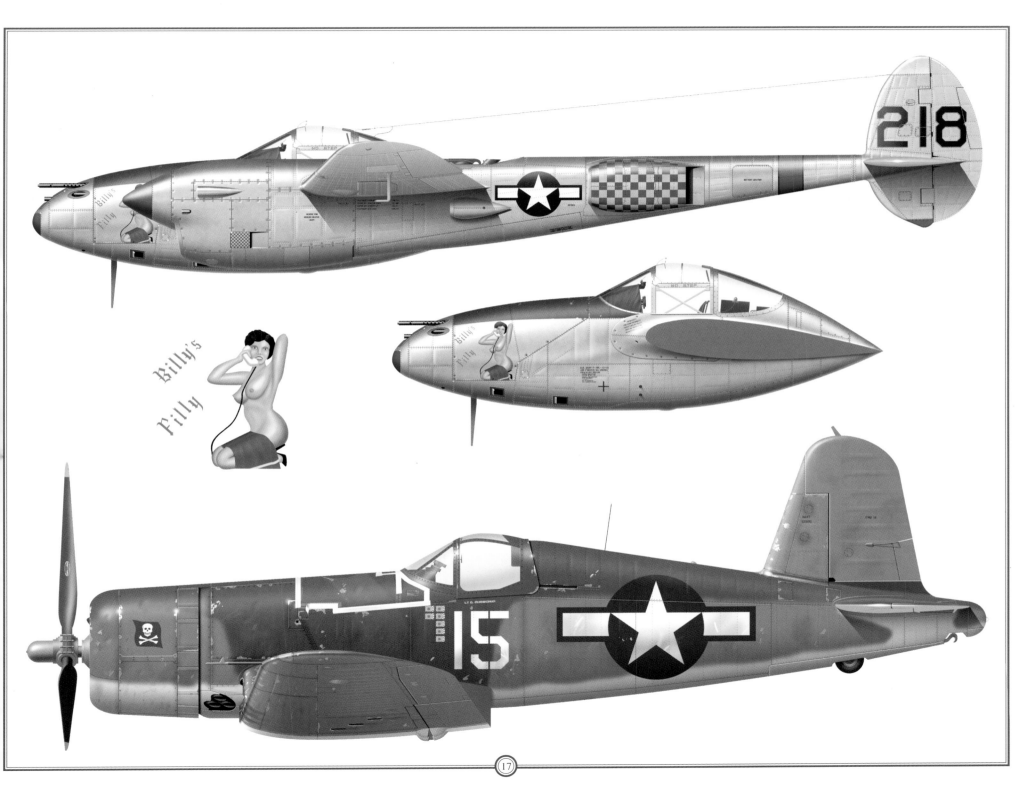

Billy's Filly

Vought F4U-1D

USS Franklin • 25 March 1945

Notes:

While this aircraft was originally based on the USS Franklin (and carried the Franklin's markings), it was eventually moved to the USS Yorktown after USS Franklin was taken out of action by Kamikaze attacks.

Colors:
Standard U.S. Navy Glossy Sea Blue scheme
Prop Blades: Black with Yellow tips

References:
F4U Corsair in action (original edition) by Jim Sullivan. Squadron Signal Publications, 1977.

Lockheed P-38J

Major Donald Campbell • 36th FS, 8th FG • 1944

Colors:
Overall natural metal with some areas painted aluminum
Prop Blades: Black with Yellow tips
Anti-glare panel: Black

References:
Attack & Conquer: The 8th Fighter Group in WWII by John Stanaway. Schiffer Publishing, 1995.

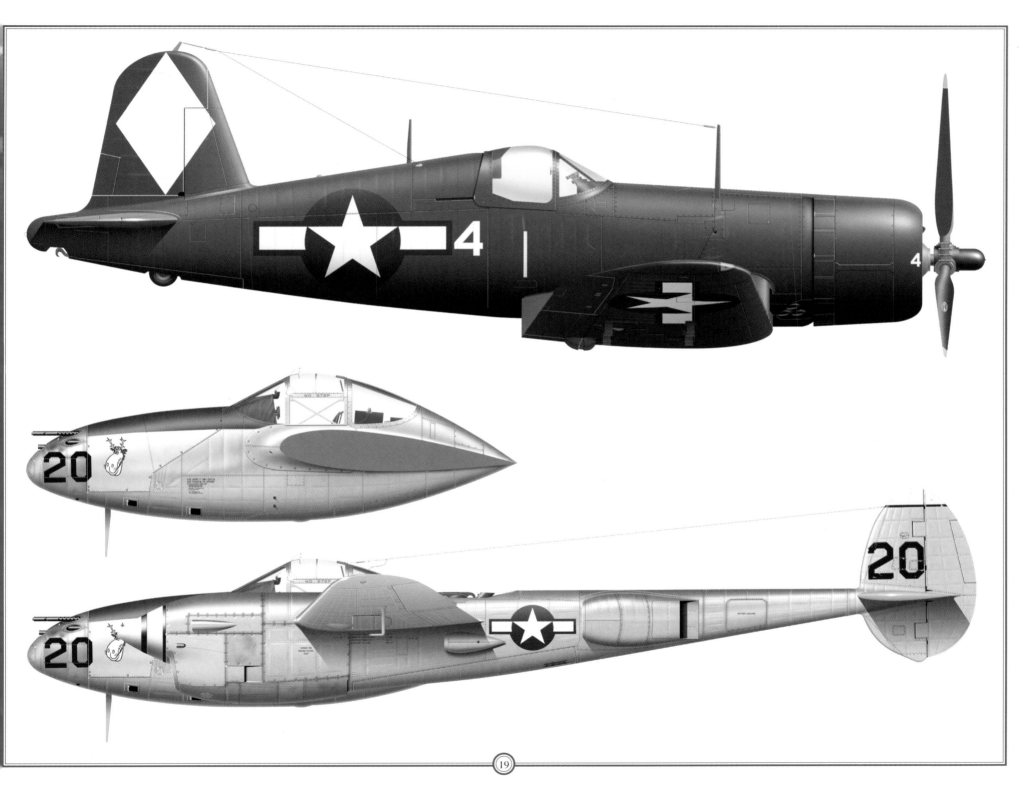

Lockheed P-38J-15

42-103921 • Lt. Richard E. West • 35th FS, 8th FG • July 1944

Colors:
Overall natural metal with some areas painted aluminum
Prop Blades: Black with Yellow tips
Anti-glare panel: Black

References:
Attack & Conquer: The 8th Fighter Group in WWII by John Stanaway. Schiffer Publishing, 1995.

Curtiss Hawk H81A-2 (P-40B)

Fin # P-8147
Erik Schilling • 2nd Pursuit Squadron, American Volunteer Group (A.V.G.) • China • 1941

Notes:
The upper surface pattern was applied using rubber templates resulting in a fairly hard edged camouflage similar to RAF fighters.
This aircraft was converted to a photo recon platform by removing the wing guns and cutting a 10"
hole in the bottom of the fuselage (directly under access hatch mid fuselage) for camera.
For their group's courage, duty, innovation, and tenacity in the face of adversity, the AVG Flying Tigers were the recipients of the
National Aviation Hall of Fame's 1999 "Milton Caniff Spirit of Flight Award."

Colors:
Undersurfaces: Sky (actually a DuPont color which was a cool grey with a slight bluish-green hue-not a very good match for the British Sky color)
Uppersurfaces: Dark Earth, Dark Green
Prop blades: Black with Yellow tips

References:
Original photos & interview with Erik Schilling

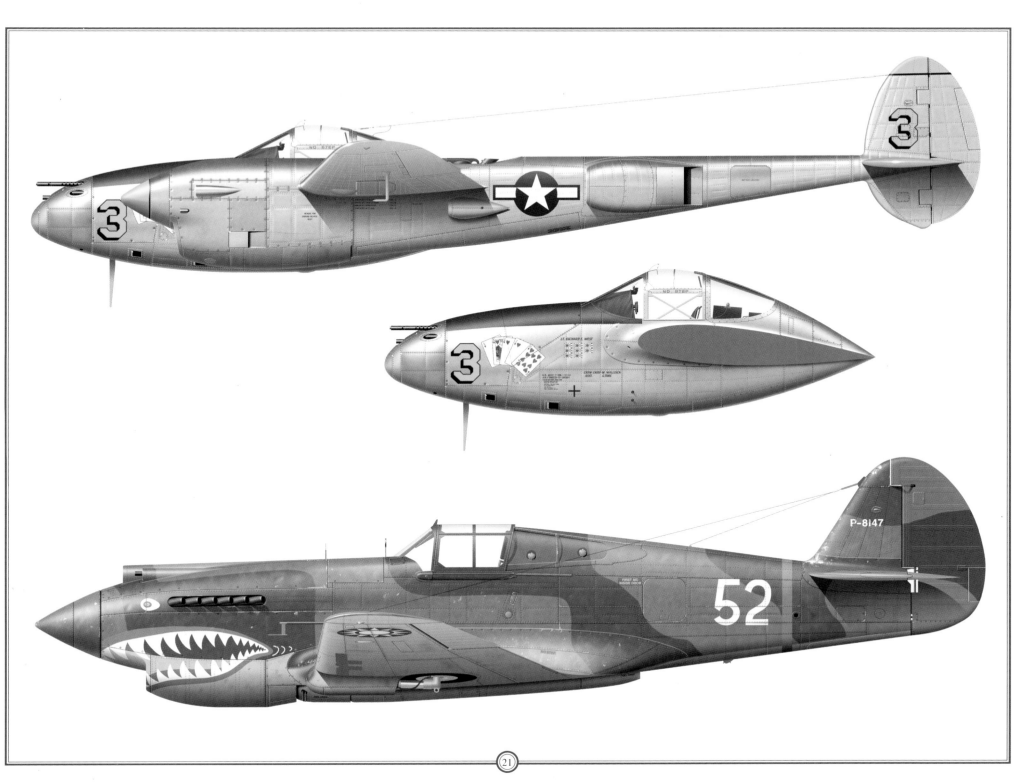

Curtiss Hawk H81A-2 (P-40B)

Fin # P-8164
Robert J. Sandell, Squadron leader • 1st Pursuit Squadron, American Volunteer Group (A.V.G.) • China • 1941

Notes:
The upper surface pattern was applied using rubber templates resulting in a fairly hard edged camouflage similar to RAF fighters.
For their group's courage, duty, innovation, and tenacity in the face of adversity, the AVG Flying Tigers were the recipients of the
National Aviation Hall of Fame's 1999 "Milton Caniff Spirit of Flight Award."

Colors:
Undersurfaces: Sky (actually a DuPont color which was a cool grey with a slight bluish-green hue-not a very good match for the British Sky color)
Uppersurfaces: Dark Earth, Dark Green
Prop blades: Black with Yellow tips

References:
Original photo
Magazine clipping (original magazine unknown)

Vought F4U-1A

"Big Hog" • Lt. Cdr. Tom Blackburn Squadron C.O. • VF-17 • November 1943 • Ondongo, New Georgia

Notes:
"What a big hog!" was Blackburn's first comment upon seeing his first F4U, and thus originated the name for his Corsair.
Note patches on mid-fuselage covering bullet holes.

Colors:
Standard U.S. Navy tri-color scheme consisting of Non Specular Sea Blue, Intermediate Blue and Non Specular White
Prop Blades: Black with Yellow tips
Spinner: Insignia Red

References:
Original photos from the collection of Jerry Crandall
Interview with Tom Blackburn conducted by Jerry Crandall

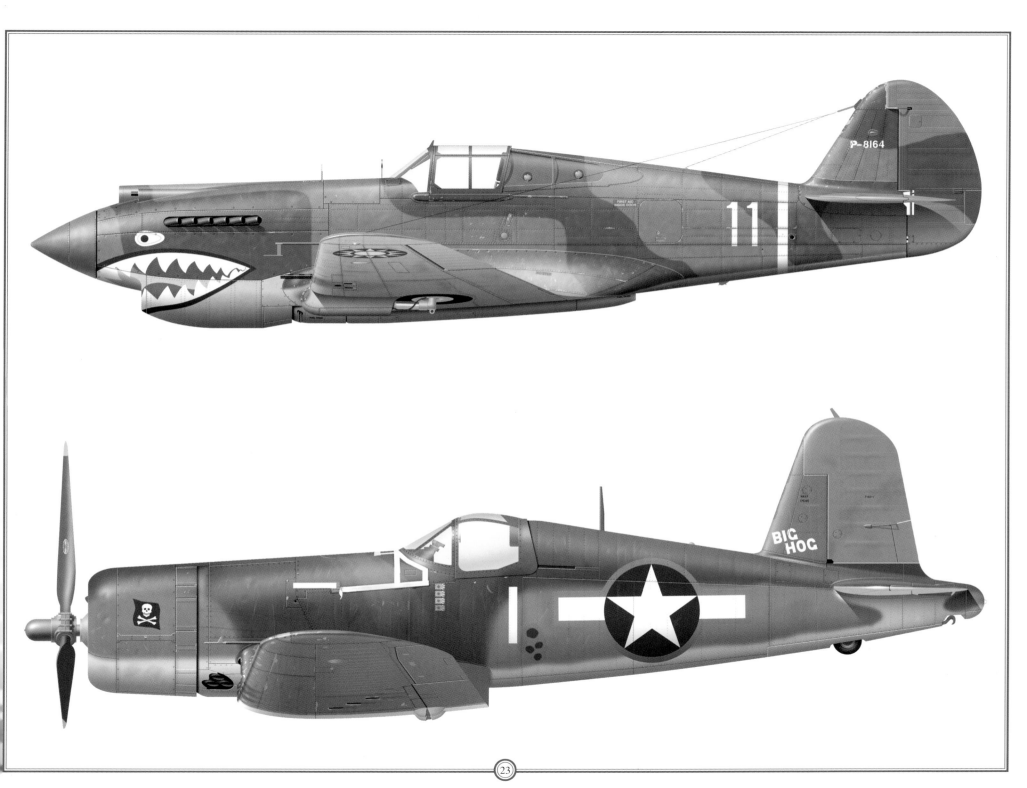

Goodyear FG-1D

"SKIPPER'S ORCHID" • HQSS-22 (Headquarters Service Squadron) • Ie Shima, Ryukyu Islands • June 1945

Colors:
Standard U.S. Navy Glossy Sea Blue scheme
Prop Blades: Black with Yellow tips

References:
Original Photo

Curtiss P-40B

18th Pursuit Group • Wheeler Field, Hawaii • 7 December 1941

Notes:
Underwing "U.S. ARMY" was actually Insignia Blue, not Black as often depicted.

Colors:
Undersurfaces: Neutral Gray
Uppersurfaces: Olive Drab
Prop blades: Black with Yellow tips

References:
Airpower magazine, January 2000.

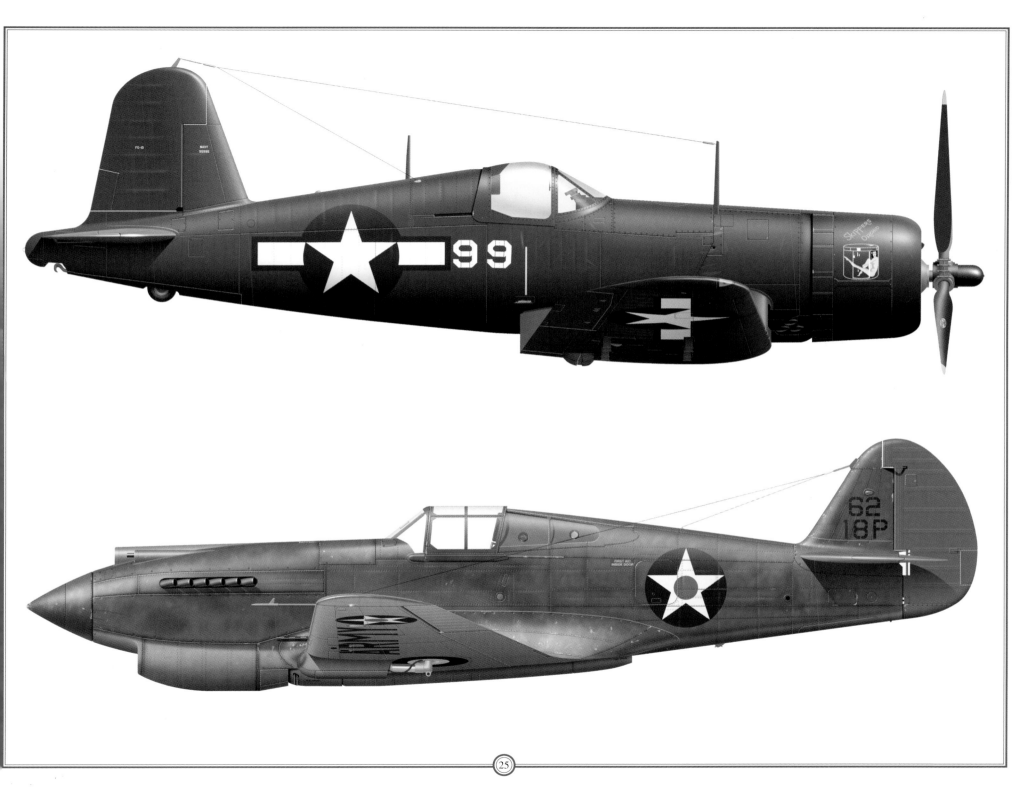

Curtiss P-40B

18th Pursuit Group • Bellows Field, Hawaii • 7 December 1941

Notes:
Underwing 'U.S. ARMY' was actually Insignia Blue, not Black as often depicted.

Colors:
Undersurfaces: Neutral Gray
Uppersurfaces: Olive Drab
Prop blades: Black with Yellow tips

References:
Airpower magazine, January 2000.

Grumman F4F-4

Captain Marion Carl • VMF-223 • Guadalcanal • September 1942

Colors:
Standard U.S. Navy two tone scheme consisting of Blue Gray over Light Gray
Prop Blades: Black with Yellow tips

References:
Marine Fighting Squadron One-Twenty-One by Thomas Doll. 1996 Squadron Signal Publications
Wildcat Aces of WWII by Barrett Tillman. Osprey Publishing, 1995.

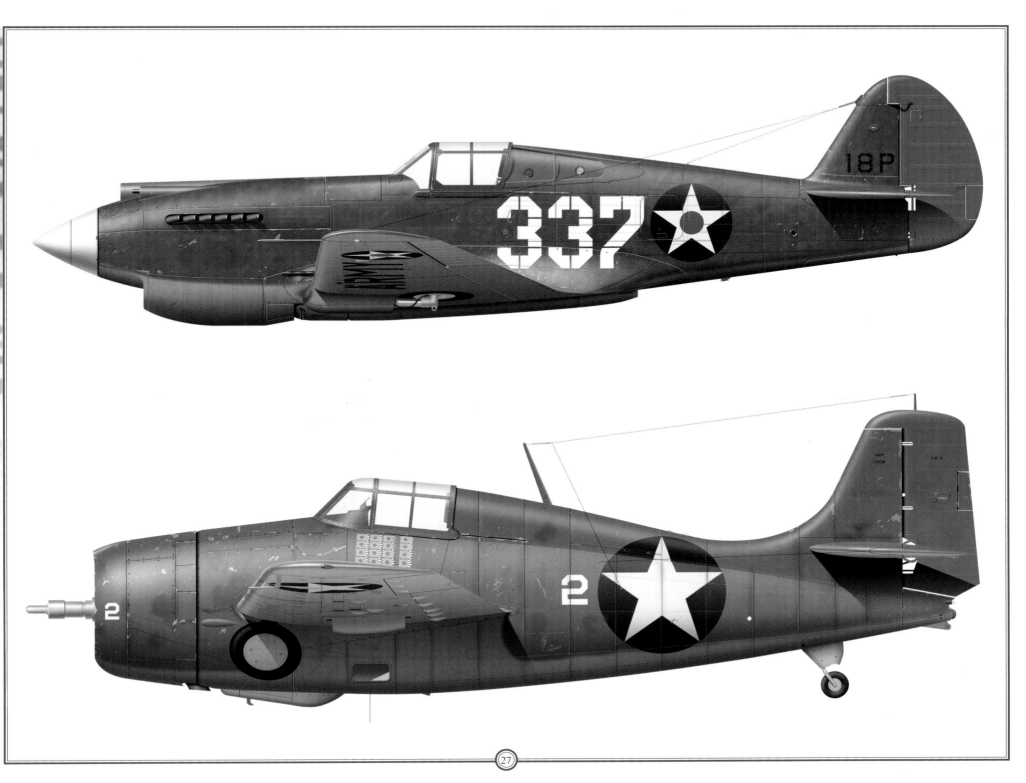

Curtiss Hawk H81A-2 (P-40B)

Fin # P-8133
Tommy Haywood • 3rd Pursuit Squadron, American Volunteer Group (A.V.G.) • China • 1941

Notes:
The upper surface pattern was applied using rubber templates resulting in a fairly hard edged camouflage similar to RAF fighters.
The bulldog insignia was added by Haywood as a reference to his days as a USMC pilot.
Later the aircraft had the bulldog removed and a Hell's Angel insignia applied on the port fuselage.
For their group's courage, duty, innovation, and tenacity in the face of adversity, the AVG Flying Tigers were the recipients of the
National Aviation Hall of Fame's 1999 "Milton Caniff Spirit of Flight Award."

Colors:
Undersurfaces: Sky (actually a DuPont color which was a cool gray with a slight bluish-green hue-not a very good match for the British Sky color)
Uppersurfaces: Dark Earth, Dark Green
Prop blades: Black with Yellow tips

References:
Original photos

Grumman F4F-4

Lt. James Swett • VMF-221 • Guadalcanal

Notes:
While Swett was confident that aircraft '77' was the one that carried his caveman art on the tail, he was not 100% sure.
The art was only carried for a couple of days before Swett was ordered to remove it.
Note the painted-out stripe on the tail/rudder. The dark sprayed color used to cover the stripe appears to be fresh Blue Gray.
This F4F has an unusual antenna arrangement on the vertical tail.

Colors:
Standard U.S. Navy two tone scheme consisting of Blue Gray over Light Gray
Prop Blades: Black with Yellow tips
Antenna Mast: White tip on Blue Gray mast.

References:
Interview with Jim Swett
Photos provided by Jay Ashurst
Research assistance provided by Ron Kaplan

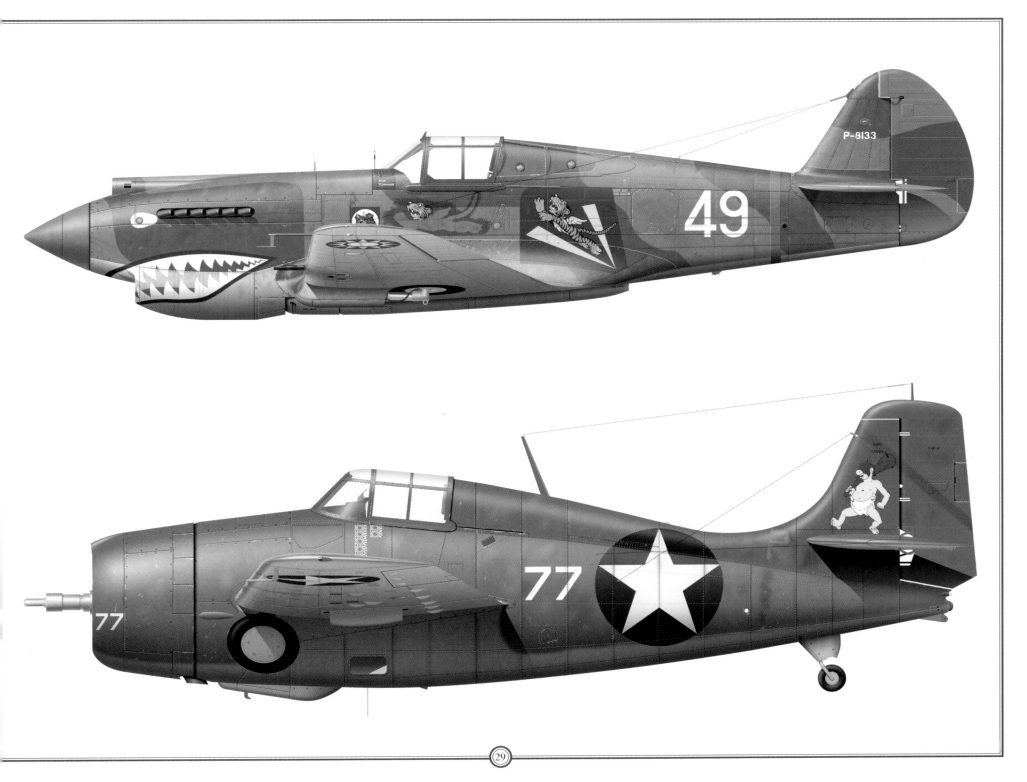

Curtiss P-40C

78th Pursuit Squadron, 18th Pursuit Group • Bellows Field, Hawaii • December 1941

Notes:
Underwing 'U.S. ARMY' was actually Insignia Blue, not Black as often depicted.
Rudder shows evidence of having been repainted, perhaps to cover early rudder stripes.
In the photo, the fuselage roundel appears not to have the red center dot. Under careful examination, the dot can just barely be seen. I believe this to
simply be a matter of the sun glaring off of the roundel, and not the center dot being painted out, as that order would come many months later.

Colors:
Undersurfaces: Neutral Gray
Uppersurfaces: Olive Drab
Prop blades: Black with Yellow tips

References:
P-40 Hawks at War by J. Christy & J. Ethell. Charles Scribner's Sons, 1980.

Vought F4U-1A

Lt. Stout • VMF-422

Notes:
This is a modified version of the profile that appeared in Eagles Illustrated #1. Since the publication of that volume,
new photos of this aircraft have been obtained by the artist and the additional information has been incorporated into the illustration.

Colors:
Standard U.S. Navy tri-color scheme consisting of Non Specular Sea Blue, Intermediate Blue and Non Specular White
Prop Blades: Black with Yellow tips

References:
Original photos from the collection of Jim Sullivan

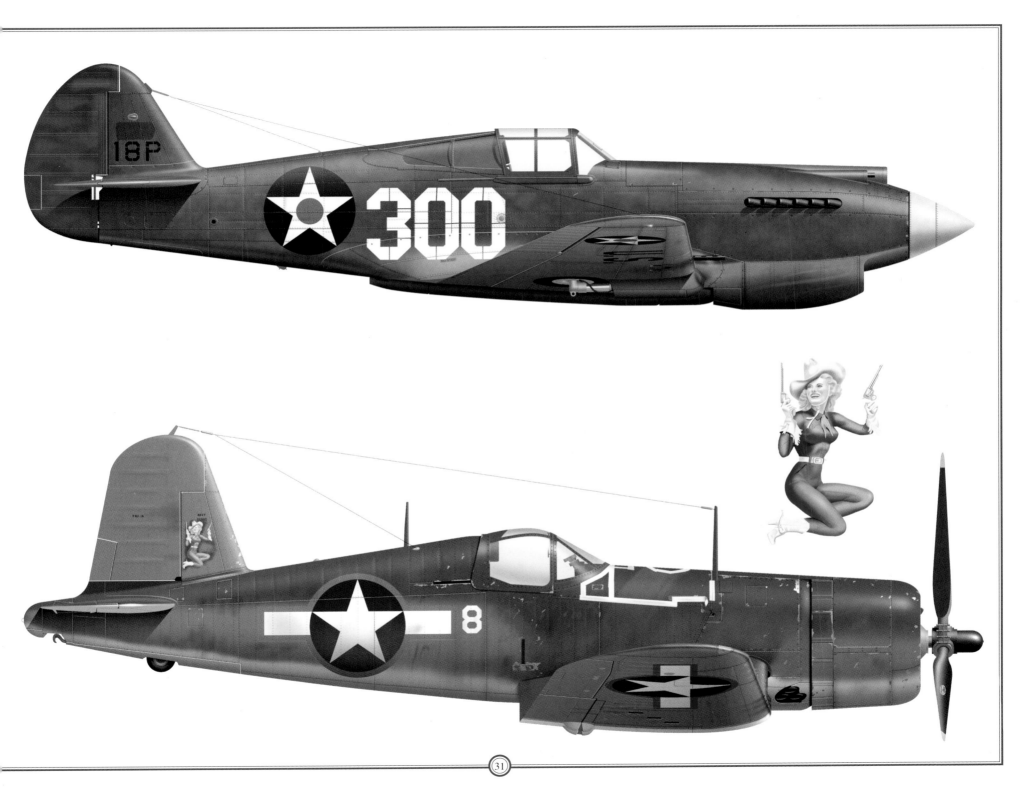

Curtiss Hawk H81A-2 (P-40B)

Fin # P-8125
Peter Atkinson • 1st Pursuit Squadron, American Volunteer Group (A.V.G.) • China • 1941

Notes:
The upper surface pattern was applied using rubber templates resulting in a fairly hard edged camouflage similar to RAF fighters.
This is the way the original 100 aircraft appeared when they were delivered to China.
For their group's courage, duty, innovation, and tenacity in the face of adversity, the AVG Flying Tigers were the recipients of the
National Aviation Hall of Fame's 1999 "Milton Caniff Spirit of Flight Award."

Colors:
Undersurfaces: Sky
Uppersurfaces: Dark Earth, Dark Green
Prop blades: Black with Yellow tips

References:
The Pictorial History of the Flying Tigers by Larry M. Pistole. Moss Publications, 1981.

Lockheed P-38L-5

44-25600 • Elliot Summer • 432dn FS, 475th FG • 1945

Colors:
Overall natural metal with some areas painted aluminum
Prop Blades: Black with Yellow tips
Anti-glare panel: Olive Drab

References:
Possum, Clover & Hades: The 475th Fighter Group in WWII by John Stanaway. Schiffer Publishing, 1993.
Interview with John Stanaway.

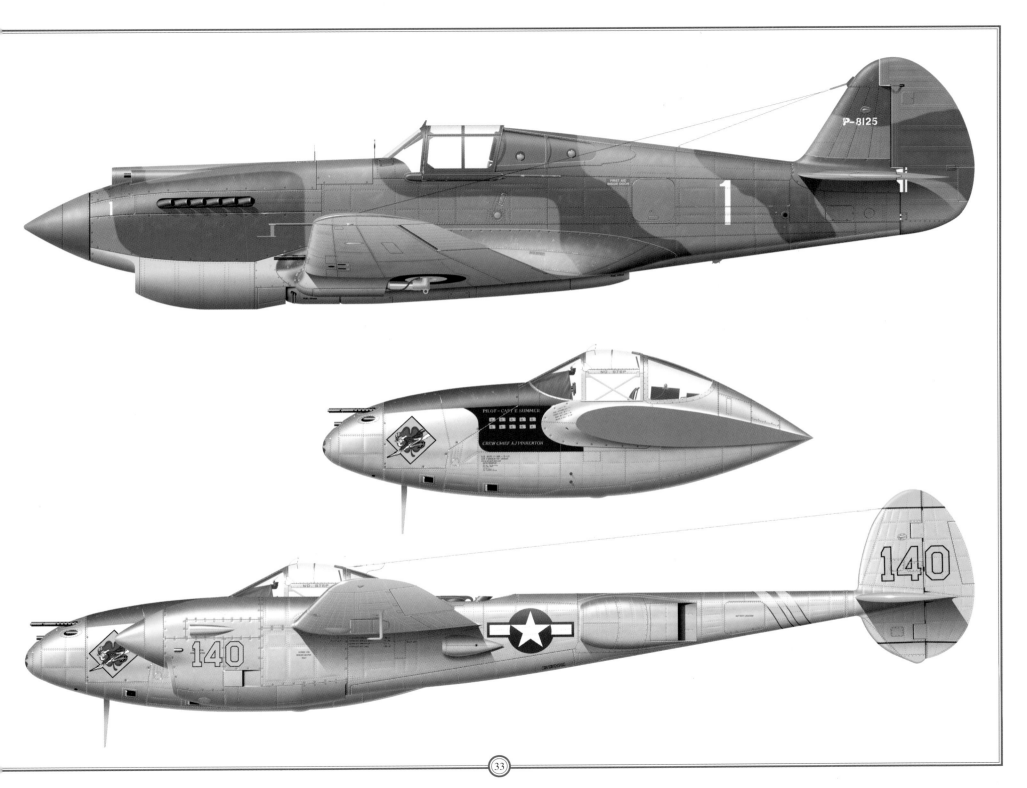

Vought F4U-1A

NZ5393 • RNZAF • Guadalcanal • 1944

Notes:
Note the dark paint that has been applied to various positions along the fuselage. This has been interpreted as a Dark Blue, similar to that used by the U.S. Navy.
While many F4Us in the RNZAF retained their U.S. Navy colors, some RNZAF Corsairs were repainted in a medium Blue Gray color over Light Gray.

Colors:
Fuselage & Wings: Blue Gray over Light Gray.
Prop Blades: Black with Yellow tips

References:
Corsair Aces of World War 2 by Mark Styling. Osprey Publishing, 1995.
F4U Corsair, Monografie #11. A-J Press, 1993.

Vought F4U-1

VMF-213

Notes:
Only the mid fuselage was visible in the reference photo (from the '38' to just forward of the head artwork).
The remainder of the aircraft is based on other F4U-1s.

Colors:
Standard U.S. Navy two tone scheme consisting of Blue Gray over Light Gray
Prop Blades: Black with Yellow tips

References:
Original photo provided by Jim Sullivan.

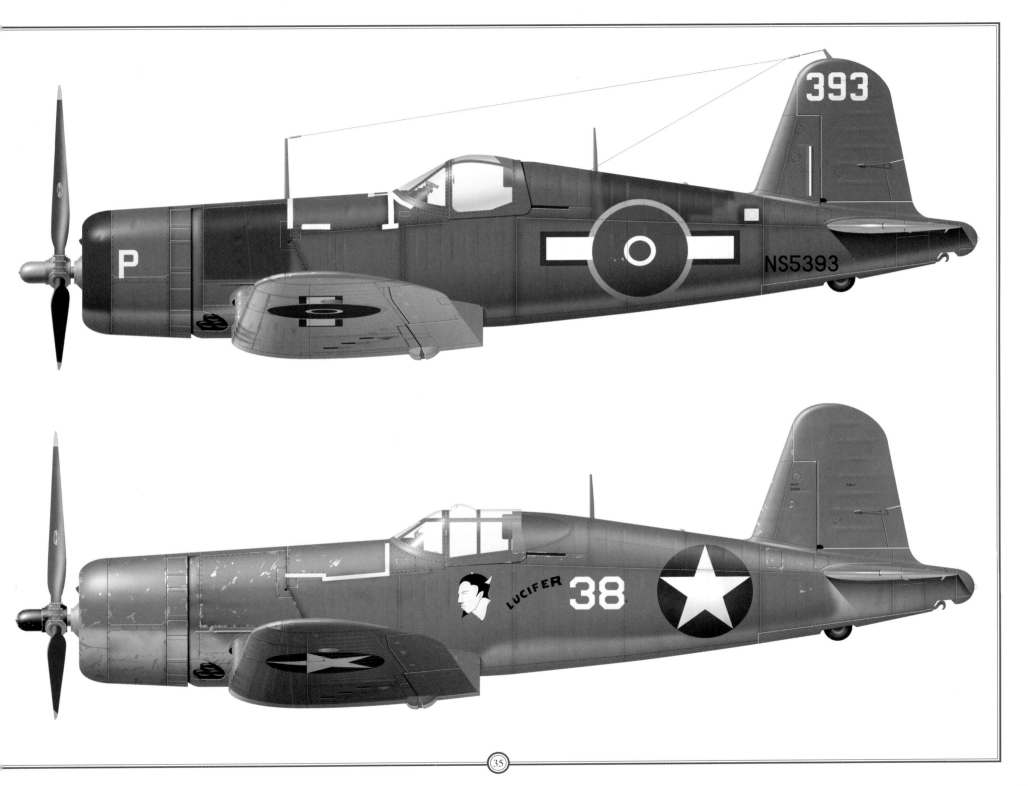

Curtiss Hawk H81A-2 (P-40B)

Fin # P-8184
Peter Wright, Flight leader • 2nd Pursuit Squadron, American Volunteer Group (A.V.G.) • China • 1941

Notes:
The upper surface pattern was applied using rubber templates resulting in a fairly hard edged camouflage similar to RAF fighters.
The shark mouth is provisional as no photos of port shark mouth could be found and is based on a photo of the starboard mouth.
This illustration was originally commissioned by Peter Wright for his family. Only one photo of this H81A-2 could be found, but it was a shot of it after a crash landing, taken at a distance, from the starboard side. Peter provided detailed notes and a sketch to aid in my rendering his aircraft, and until additional photos surface this should be considered the definitive depiction of his Tomahawk.
For their group's courage, duty, innovation, and tenacity in the face of adversity, the AVG Flying Tigers were the recipients of the National Aviation Hall of Fame's 1999 "Milton Caniff Spirit of Flight Award."

Colors:
Undersurfaces: Sky
Uppersurfaces: Dark Earth, Dark Green
Prop blades: Black with Yellow tips

References:
Original photo & interviews with Peter Wright

Vought F4U-1D

VMF-441 • 1945

Colors:
Standard U.S. Navy Glossy Sea Blue scheme
Prop Blades: Black with Yellow tips
Spinner and Forward Cowl: Light Blue

References:
F4U Corsair in action (new edition) by Jim Sullivan. Squadron Signal Publications, 1994.

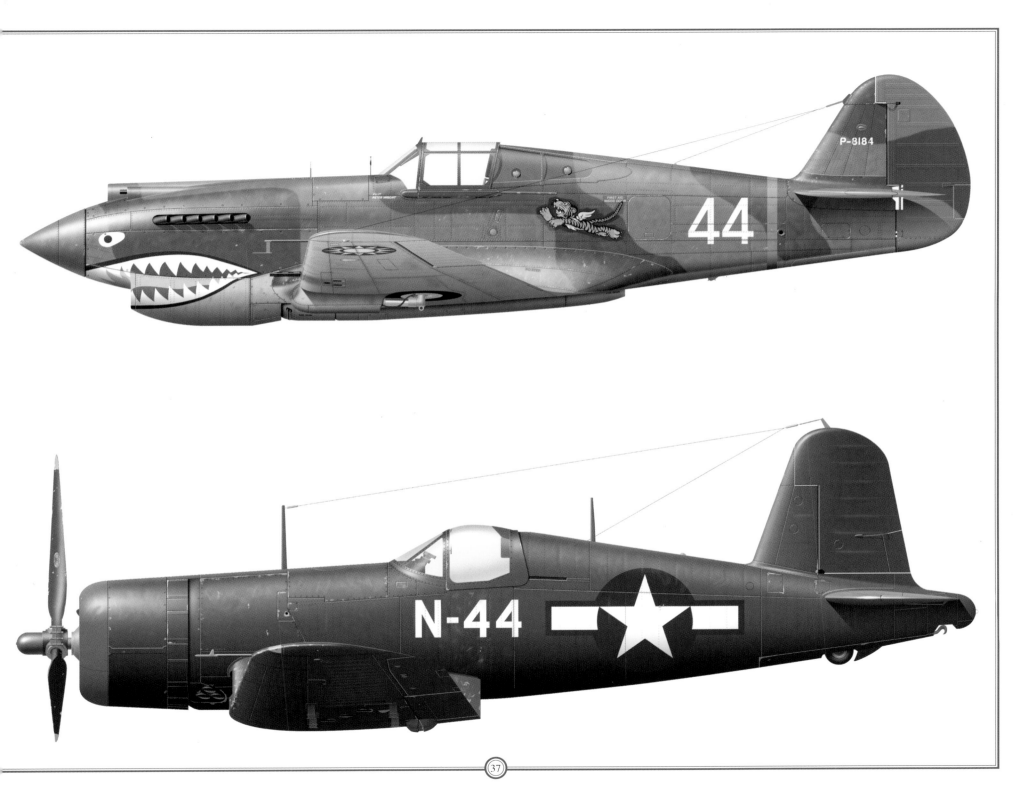

Vought F4U-1D

VBF-83 • USS Essex • Spring 1945

Notes:
Note oversprayed edges from masking tape used for painting tail carrier marking.
This F4U-1D has the old-style braced canopy that was common to F4U-1A Corsairs.

Colors:
Standard U.S. Navy Glossy Sea Blue scheme
Prop Blades: Black with Yellow tips
Forward Cowl: White

References:
F4U Corsair in action (new edition) by Jim Sullivan. Squadron Signal Publications, 1994.

Curtiss Hawk H81A-2 (P-40B)

Fin # P-8121
Ken Jernstedt • 3rd Pursuit Squadron, American Volunteer Group (A.V.G.) • China • 1941

Notes:
The upper surface pattern was applied using rubber templates resulting in a fairly hard edged camouflage similar to RAF fighters.
The only known photo of this aircraft showed just the cockpit area with the Hell's Angel insignia, pilot's name and kill markings.
The rest of the aircraft was reconstructed from Jernstedt's exceptional memory and other aircraft with similar fuselage numbers (87, 89, etc.)
For their group's courage, duty, innovation, and tenacity in the face of adversity, the AVG Flying Tigers were the recipients of the
National Aviation Hall of Fame's 1999 "Milton Caniff Spirit of Flight Award."

Colors:
Undersurfaces: Sky
Uppersurfaces: Dark Earth, Dark Green
Prop blades: Black with Yellow tips

References:
Original photo
Interview & notes from Ken Jernstedt

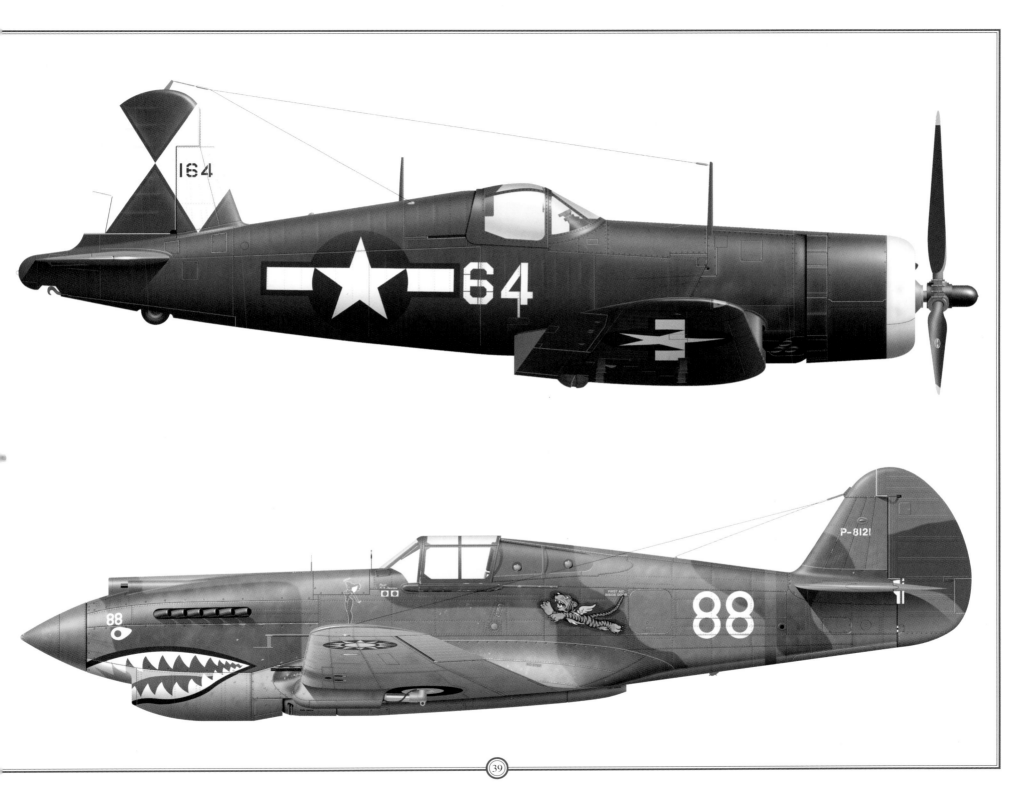

Next in the series:

Eagles Illustrated Vol. 3 'Guardians of the Reich'

Approximately 40 full color Luftwaffe aircraft.

First in this exciting series:

Eagles Illustrated Vol. 1 'Fighters of WWII'

Approximately 40 full color WWII aircraft.